Mother Mary on the Light

THE TEMPLE OF THE PRESENCE®

The Ascended Master Wisdom delivered by
Monroe Julius Shearer & Carolyn Louise Shearer

Mother Mary:
On the Light

Published by
Acropolis Sophia Books & Works®
an imprint of
The Temple of The Presence®
P.O. Box 17839, Tucson, Arizona 85731

www.TempleofThePresence.org

Copyright © 1997, 1998, 2016, 2020 The Temple of The Presence, Inc.
All rights reserved.
No part of this book may be reproduced
in any form or by any means whatsoever without prior
written permission, except in the case of brief quotations
embodied in articles and reviews.

For information, write
Acropolis Sophia Books & Works®
P.O. Box 17839, Tucson, Arizona 85731

Printed in the United States of America
First Printing, 2020
ISBN: 978-1-7337302-3-5

Table of Contents

Letter from the Anointed Representatives® 2

The Mother Light and Your Ascension 5

Honoring the First Commandment 15

Find Your Refuge in the Light of God 27

Rosaries to Mother Mary 41

Beloved Students,

In the enfolding Radiance of the Light, you are invited into the Heart of Beloved Mary. If you are a student of the Ascended Masters, you know this glorious Ascended Being as Mother Mary, Archeia of the Fifth Ray. If you come from the heritage of the Christian Faith, you know her as the Mother of Jesus or as Mary, Queen of the Angels. You have called upon her often for intercession, for Healing and Wholeness.

As Archeia of the Fifth Ray, Mother Mary brings the Light of the Emerald Matrix to the Sons and Daughters of God and holds them in the Immaculate Concept of their Christhood. With her entourage of Angels, she often stands beside you, enfolding you in her Love and assisting you in becoming the Christ.

It is our hope that as you read through Mother Mary's Teaching in this pocketbook series, you will become closer to your own God Presence and learn to bring a greater momentum of Godliness, Wholeness, and Light into your life. For the secret ingredient is, and always has been, the Light of God. The Light of God comes in many forms, from many directions, but ultimately it is All One — the One Light of God's Presence.

We, likewise, hope that you will be empowered to walk the Path to Christhood as Beloved Jesus did and that you will find the Love of your Heart propelling you forward toward your own Ascension in the Light.

We have known Beloved Mother Mary throughout the ages. This is not our first lifetime in close communion with her Presence. In preparation for our Mission as Anointed Representatives for the Brotherhood of Light, Beloved Carolyn was embodied as Saint Bernadette. And now once again, she speaks on behalf of Mother Mary, sharing her Message and Teaching with the world.

We invite you to enter into the Heart of the Queen of Angels, into the Light and Current of the Emerald Ray as you walk the pathway home to God in Victory and in Love. Know that you are loved beyond measure within the embrace of this glorious Ascended Mother of Heaven.

In the Grace of the Heart of Mary,

Monroe Julius Shearer & *Carolyn Louise Shearer*

Anointed Representatives®
The Temple of The Presence®

The Mother Light and Your Ascension

My Dear Children,

Can you hear the Silence? Do you perceive the Light? From the comments you have placed upon my Heart, I know there are those who would have the Fullness of the Light of God within them for their desiring is great, but the desired accomplishment has been difficult. I have felt the pain of your heart caused by the separation from that Light. But I, Mother of the Flame of Life, do take you in my arms, hold you close that you might feel the Mother Light within me and have it surge through your body temple, so that you might manifest the Mother Light where you are.

The Immaculate Concept

As the Mother of Jesus, I coddled him, nurtured him, and held the balance that he might come into his own. The Immaculate Concept, which I held for his lifestream — that Pure, Pristine, Essential Vision that he was the Christ from his birth — guided and guarded him to stay on course until the Resurrection Flame burned brightly through his own Being. It is no small task to hold a single-eyed Vision, one-pointed for years and years and years. You say, "You are Mother Mary. You can do this. You have the Attainment." Blessed ones, you have the Attainment. You have been trained. You have been taught at inner levels how to hold the Immaculate Concept, not just for other lifestreams, but for your own. Yes, for yourself, beloved ones.

Your Mission begins with you. You cannot save a planet, you cannot raise the Light in others until it is raised in your own temple. While you can talk about high ideals and guide a person to this or that, becoming the example is always the greatest teacher. By conserving the Light of the Cosmic Christ within your temple, you are able to ignite those whom you contact. Then, as you walk, talk, and fulfill your dharma, you will be blessing all of life wherever you go. This is the Mission. This is the genuine Grail Quest. You hold the goal in your mind. You maintain the Immaculate Concept, but it is in actively pursuing this Quest that you win your Victory each day.

Be the Mother Light

By the time all of Heaven opens for you, you will be in a state of receptive Bliss where it will not come as a surprise, with giant bells ringing out. Why, it could come as silently as the spark of an ember, realizing that this Quest is the goal. The Mother Light which you, each one, hold in your chakras must be raised. For in the union of the Light with the Father is the birth of the Christ. There cannot be one without the other.

While embodied as Mother Mary, I was very aware during my travels of the anchoring of certain Forcefields of Light for future times. This can be done by you, beloved ones. You can be a messenger of Light for a future time.

But you must have Light to deposit. It is not enough to just simply say, "I want to do good deeds. I want to bless future generations."

You must desire with all your heart, with all your soul, with all your might, that every aspect of your lifestream be filled as a Chalice of Light. I know you may stumble at times. I know there will be wrong decisions, but I pray with all my Heart and with all of the Momentum of my Causal Body Attainment that those wrong decisions will not be so grievous as to take you from your chosen path. I pray you will hold dear and ever-present this goal.

Define Your Quest

The Holy Grail became the Quest for the Knights of the Round Table. What is your Quest? Do you know how to name it? Do you know what it looks like — how to visualize it when your eyes are closed? When your mind is busy, would it be difficult for you to recreate that vision? This will take work for many, especially those who do not have a momentum in meditation, who are constantly letting their minds flit this way and that, unable to control a focal point for their experience in the Light. For many, if you could but sit and focus your attention on something beautiful just long enough, you might hear your own Presence speaking to you.

I will assist you if you will but try this exercise, and if you choose to pour out your heart to me, I will guide you, I will speak to you, but you must listen. It is not enough in this day and age of incessant comings and goings, with all the scattered vibrations of this planet flying hither and yon, for you to simply say a thing and then be on your merry way, thinking, "Well, this sign will happen and that sign will happen, and I will have my answer that I can rely on." If you have great attainment, you may be able to accomplish this. But heed my instruction — if you are serious and choose to come into the Fullness of all that you are — you must take the necessary time to ensure your outcome is the Will of God. Set aside a certain allotment of time daily to listen, to hold the vision of your goal in your third eye and make the commitment required for the Victory.

The Vision of Your Holy Christ Presence

May I tell you what you can expect once you are wearing the Mantle of your Holy Christ Presence constantly, daily? Each time you close your eyes, you will be able to see only Light, Light, Light. There will be no more darkness. There will be no more fleeting images bumping into one another in the night. Then, when there is a vision, it will have purpose and meaning for your lifestream, and you will know what that vision means.

Spiritual visions are peculiar things, dear ones. They can teach you and guide you. They can intimidate you, frighten you. They can warn you. They can evoke any record you choose to tie into. Notice I said you *choose* to tie into. One must be clear about all such visions, for the subconscious mind will play on the akashic record of your lifestream, drawing out the remaining karma to be balanced.

Then how are you to put trust in your visions? What is the sign? If you cannot simply accept everything you see, what do you look for? You look for vibration, dear ones, vibration. There must be a resonating vibration in your world that says, "YES, this is confirmed by my Holy Christ Presence. This is a vision I should attend to." The Ascended Master Vibration is a vibration you can trust. If you are engaged in worldly activities and are removed from that Vibration for a period of time and need desperately in your life to feel galvanized to the Flame again, find a Dictation, a song, a picture — something you can hold on to, to move back into the remembrance of the Release of Ascended Master Light. Let this Charge of Light be the guidepost so you will have something to compare to your own vibration. You will remember what has caused a Release of Light in your world so great that it was able to reach through the veils of maya and leave such a record that you could now pull upon.

The Mother Light Leads to the Light of the Father

Reaching for the goal, striving for the Light, being the Mother Flame in Action — these will guide you all the way to your Ascension in the Light. You can be a Christ, right here today. Allow the Fires to burn brightly. Do not squander one erg of precious Light, for you know not "when the well might run dry." Oh yes, there is Cosmic Light released, and there is a certain nourishment you will receive from that Cosmic Light daily. It will benefit and bless your lifestream for many embodiments. But you cannot make your Ascension, beloved ones — you cannot be released from the wheel of karma — without the Mother Light. It is essential to making your Ascension.

Until you master this Light, you will stay on the wheel of karma. And even though there are those of you who would stay in embodiment with the justification of blessing mankind, I tell you, you take great risks, greater than most should undertake. For you know not whether the next embodiment will be in a place where you will have so great an opportunity to win your Ascension. You will bless more of mankind, nourish more of life, and expand more Light by gaining your Ascension.

I will hold the Immaculate Concept for you. Recorded on my Heart are those requests of the children of the Light who desire my assistance. Many of you have been calling to me for many embodiments. You have served my Flame well with great Devotion. Now I ask you to serve the Mother Light within you as well. Raise that Light and be filled with Light.

As a Mother, I want to tell you every little nuance to look for, to do, to guide you. But there also comes a time when, as the Mother, I am compelled to stand back and let you experience the Light of your own Flame. I was compelled to do this with Jesus. I still held the Immaculate Concept for him and guided him from afar. But there came a time when he had to be entrusted, fully and completely, to the Father.

I will guide you and protect you as you reach for the Light of the Father to become the Christ.

Yours devotedly,

Mother Mary

Honoring the First Commandment

I bow my head to the Presence of the Light of God. I serve the Light. I worship the Light. I AM Mary, Devoted Mother of the Light. From the time I became a devotee of the Light, while going through my own incarnations and walking the steps you walk, I turned my attention to God. My Heart was only filled when I was thinking of God. In my embodiment as the Mother of Jesus, when I was but three, I felt the Holy Angels winging the Love of God to my Heart, entertaining my every need. I knew even then that what was giving me Joy and Upliftment, Courage and Strength, and most of all Comfort was the Love of God.

Thus Devotion to the Flame became my whole life. As I prepared for my Mission, my attention was only upon the Flame of God. Through that

Flame, I was able to outpicture all of the good that was necessary in holding the Immaculate Concept for my Beloved Jesus. Had I not been devoted to the Love of God as the Bride of the Bridegroom, I would not have had the Strength, the Courage or the Fortitude to carry out that Mission.

Put God First in Your Relationships

You have many relationships throughout a lifetime, and if you were to count your many incarnations, your relationships would number in the tens of thousands and more. When you consider the Devotion, the attention, and the Love you have given to those lifestreams, it has been great. How many can say that their Devotion and attention to God have been as great? You see, you have looked at your life with God and others completely backwards. For any relationship to be enriched and full, you must first possess the Light of God within yourself.

If you had placed your attention upon the Heart of the Beloved God Self, had you nourished that Flame first, you would have found enrichment and fulfillment in all your relationships. You would have found an attunement to keep you in alignment with the correct relationships, for many have squandered precious hours and days. Many of you have wasted entire embodiments, entangled in relationships that were simply no more than maya and illusion — surely not based in God Reality. You did not even balance your previous karma with those lifestreams; you created even more karma. Had your attention and Devotion been first and foremost on God, you would have had the clarity and the understanding of the right use of the Light of your Heart.

Have you ever thought why you do not wish to mingle with certain individuals that you come in contact with? What keeps you at a distance from some and not others? Is it because you do not like the way they look or the way they act? Or does it go deeper? Is it more a consideration of their vibration? If the vibration of your heart is accustomed to being coddled within the Heart of God, do you not think that those you choose to surround yourself with will have a like vibration?

Thereby, you gain the opportunity for creating God Good and for outpicturing the Fullness of the Divine Plan that can be afforded by each of your lifestreams, unlike the reverse way of finding the relationships first, then finding God and discovering that you collectively have such karma between you that the excess baggage makes you wish you had not entered into such a relationship.

All is not lost, however. For you do have the Violet Flame, and this can help you through all of these entanglements. But, from this point forward, why not change the habits of your previous activities and follow the First Commandment: "Thou shalt have no other God before Me." God is a very jealous God. He wants your full and undivided attention. He is most willing to share you with the God within other individuals, but not willing to allow for the very Heart of your God Presence to be anchored into the physical and wasted upon anything less than the Highest Vibration of God Love.

This may seem to be a very drastic Teaching. For some will consider their lives and wonder, "Where is the fun? Where is the enjoyment?" Those who must ask this question have not felt the Love of God. For anyone who has truly entered into a state of Prayer and Devotion to God and felt the return current knows only the fulfillment of all desires and the joyous acceleration and acceptance of the Light within their being.

It matters not the relationships that you are in currently, for you may still bring the Activity of God into your world. But I will caution you. For there will be a separation from some of those you have formerly called "friends" or "loved ones," for not all have the same awakening and desire for God at the same time. You may talk to, you may study with, and you may pray and decree for those individuals. You may hold a high place for them, surrounding them with all of the Holy Angels that the Great Law will allow, and they may still turn away.

Do not be sad. Do not be concerned that these lifestreams are not ready to feel that Oneness with God you have had the opportunity to experience. It is only a matter of considering their timetables. For each lifestream is given opportunity at certain increments in life during each incarnation.

For some, as you have been told, there are repeated opportunities, and the doorways are held open for long periods of time. But for others the time has grown short because they have received much opportunity. You know not the hour or the day that further opportunity will cease for any lifestreams in that incarnation.

If you wish to be of service to those lifestreams, hold the Immaculate Concept for them. Hold them dear. See the Light of their own God Presence within your third eye. Nourish that God Presence with the Love and Devotion from your own God Presence, and you can rest assured that all will be well. For the Hand of God will have helped them along on their own path.

No two individuals have attained to the same level at the same time. There can be no idolatrous attachment to any lifestream, whether it be your Twin Flame or a karmic entanglement. For I tell you, beloved ones, you — and only you — will step into the Ascension Flame and be reunited with your God Presence for eternity. No one goes with you. It is a singular Initiation. And if the Ascension is the goal you choose to pursue, the prerequisite is Devotion to God, first and foremost. All other loves must be secondary.

Emulate a Child's Pure Love

Think for a moment about those children who naturally, at a very young age, enjoy their evening prayers, kneel by the bed with folded hands and call for a blessing for many. If you will listen to the Prayers of such a child, you will learn. For many times they will call for a Blessing from God to a part of life that you, as an adult, have overlooked or thought unimportant.

Beloved ones, the Devotion of the child is to be envied, to be emulated, to be desired. For a child knows only the pure intent. For the pure intent of the Love of God is what is necessary for the true devotee on the Path to become One with God. If you wish Healing, Wholeness, the Abundant Life, if you wish Love surrounding all of your relationships, if you wish to be One with God, then kneel in Prayer and heartfelt Devotion to your own God Presence. For that Light will fill your world, and you will not be concerned whether this person or that, or this part of life or that, is responding to the Light of God.

Offering Spiritual Nourishment Versus Doing "Good"

My dear ones, when you are filled with the Light of God, the world is beautiful, whole, and complete. This does not mean that you remain ignorant of the desecration that is taking place all around you. But it does mean that your life is filled, and in being filled you have something to offer, to give to that part of life in need. If you are not complete and whole, you have nothing to give. If your giving is in the Fullness of God, your reward will come from God, and you will be unattached to the fruit of your action. But if your giving is strictly for the cause of the outer self and you do not, first and foremost, have the Light of God flowing through you, you may still manage to accomplish a great worldly task. You may even work a great work. But, as has been taught by Krishna, your reward will be but an earthly one.

There have been many upon the planet who, lifetime after lifetime, have engaged themselves in fulfilling what they felt was good for the planet. They involve themselves in all manner of charitable activities. And, in fact, in the social circles of many of the countries there has been great good accomplished. But the enlightening of a planet, the enlightening of mankind, does not come from merely living a "good life." It does not stop with enjoying the comforts of life, being well-fed, being healthy. No, this is not what raises mankind into a Golden Age, albeit, it would appear that all are prospering and doing well.

True spiritual nourishment has been forgotten, and without spiritual nourishment, there is no lasting Peace within the physical being of a lifestream. A sense of well-being garnered outside of the Daily Bread of Life that only comes from the Source of Life only lasts for a time and maybe even for only an embodiment. But as that lifestream reincarnates, they discover that they have not really advanced far from where they began, perhaps ten thousand years before.

If you wish to help mankind, if you wish the children of God to have the nourishment, the comfort, the warmth, and the surcease from battle, then give the Sons and Daughters of God the meat of the Law and the Elixir of the Life of God. You can only give this if you are devoted to God.

Remember and Embody These Words

I trust you will not simply take my words, listen to or read them, have them pass through you, only to find that tomorrow or the next day you have forgotten the intent of my Message. For I will continue to repeat this Message until there are sufficient lifestreams who embody the Devotion to God. I do not wish to see my children of the Light hunger and thirst. I wish the Communion Cup to be offered in the form of the Light from your Heart, but you may only offer this Cup if your Heart is full.

My Heart remains full as the Constancy of a river flowing, for my gaze never leaves the Heart of God. I choose to see the God in Action within you, and I will hold the Immaculate Concept that you might fulfill your Mission. I speak not for the few, but for the many who are ready to enter into a new life, who are ready to open the door to the Heart of God. No, it is not easy at first, but the reward is great. No, there is no creature comfort in the striving, but the surcease from the battle is part of your final reward.

As you move forward and decide which way you will turn, which side of the road you will walk upon, I trust you will think about my words, and you will honor the First Commandment. Beloved ones, it was the First Commandment because of its paramount importance. Should your priorities be less?

Practice the Following Devotional Exercise Daily

I invite you to kneel where you are before the Light of your own God Presence in this hour. I ask that you place your attention upon your Heart and as the Currents of Love flow through your Heart, place your attention on the Light of your own God Presence. And if you have not as yet garnered the mastery of understanding where that Light is, place the very Love of your Heart in the atmosphere just above your head, and feel the warmth of the Light as it connects with the Light of your Heart.

This devotional exercise should be continued on a daily basis until you feel the flow of that Light into your Heart. If you find there are times when it is difficult, you may stop, give some of the calls and affirmations at your disposal, play a piece of music that will align your Heart with Devotion, and begin again. For your God Presence is always ready to receive you.

I will stand with Beloved Jesus and Beloved Saint Germain as the Holy Family to protect you as you give your Devotion. Together, We will be a Family of God, and you will have the Wholeness you desire. My Love I leave with you to draw you into the Current of the Love of God.

Mother Mary

Find Your Refuge in the Light of God

Blessed Sons and Daughters of God, Children of the Light, Far and Wide,

When you call, I, Mary, answer — not necessarily in the Office of the Mother of the Son of God, whom you have come to know as Jesus the Christ, but as the Archeia of the Fifth Ray. This Office streams forth the Presence of God as the Emerald Ray and codifies the Emerald Matrix so that you might bring to bear Necessity's Ray in your life. Wearing this Emerald Ray, radiating the Charge and the Perfection of God that streams forth, allows you to put on the Garment of the Christ, to walk straightway in Fearlessness Flame so that you are not taunted or intimidated by any appearance of unreality.

Place Your Attention Upon the Presence

When unreality raises its ugly head and tries to scare you to enter into doubt or fear, you know that you must be doing something right! It is all-important for you to understand that at the core of your being resides the Truth of the Divine Presence and the Will of God, the Wisdom of God, the Purity of God. Realize that if you are forever allowing your consciousness to entertain any lesser state of vibration than that which is held by the Mind of God within the Holy Christ Presence, then you, blessed ones, will be forever dueling with unreality, struggling through one incarnation after another and never truly reaching the goal — the Will of your God Presence to know the Purity, the Truth of Cosmic Law®, and the Divine Presence that is to manifest completely throughout all your vehicles of consciousness.

Many entertaining a Higher Path for themselves outside of the human thought and feeling that is thrust upon them from birth ofttimes will consider: Is this Path really what I should be putting my attention upon? Are these practices in accordance with the Divine Will? Do I measure up?

Am I worthy to put on this Garment of the Christ that I have been told is the Divine Plan for every Son and Daughter of God?

Those questions, blessed ones, are in order. And where do you find the answer? Right within the Flame upon the Altar of your Heart! But if there is such confusion, human doubt or fear swirling about your consciousness; agitation, anxiety, and desperation within your emotional body; or illness and pain, suffering in the physical, you must mark what is the driving cause in your life at present. What is at the helm of your decisions, your path, your way of life?

Many would like to say it is the Flame upon the Altar of their Heart. For they have listened. They have been attentive to the disciplines of Decree, Prayer, Meditation, of the Service to God in life. And they have marked their days in accordance with the priority to follow the Mighty I AM Presence. And that is all-important. However, when the pressures upon the outer vehicles, submerged beneath the weight of human conditions untransmuted, begin to swirl about and take hold of their life, they lose touch with the Flame of the Heart and must be regalvanized to that Flame for it to burn brightly once again within their consciousness, their emotional body, their physical body.

One by one, each of the vehicles of consciousness begins to be filled once more with the Light of the Mighty I AM Presence and the Ascended Masters, and there is the ability once more to overcome the lesser states of consciousness that the masses of mankind throughout the Earth feel so at home in.

You as Torch Bearers have had such a co-measurement. You have understood the Charge of the Vibration of God, the Healing Current of the Emerald Ray moving through you. Time and time again you have been witness to just such occasions and many more experiences in the Light of God. Then why would you ever fall sway to any of the misqualifications of the Light?

Certainly, within your consciousness, within your mind, you know the co-measurement, for you have said as much. Certainly, you note the records that you are able to read within those you come in contact with, the vibrations of their emotional body. You are able to judge where there is agitation in their world, or yours, and the necessity to calm the emotional body and bring Peace back into its rightful place so that the Charge of the Light from the Mighty I AM Presence has a reservoir of God Energy with which to act. That, blessed ones, is a necessity so that you can have the full Harmony required to truly be effective with the Emerald Ray and to maintain the Emerald Matrix of Perfection and Purity.

Do Not Engage in Gossip

And what of those who are constantly looking about for something negative to put their attention upon so that they might have something to speak of, to gossip about? How many times must the Sons and Daughters of God be taught that gossip is a cancerous contagion that rots the very core of the vehicle, whether it be an individual, a group of individuals, an organization, a country, the Earth?

The Sons and Daughters of God are presently living in a time when it is easier to fall into lockstep with negativity than it is to rise above it, looking to the Mighty I AM Presence for solutions, for Direction, for Healing and Wholeness. Instead, it is reminiscent of a coven born out of witchcraft in ancient times.

You, blessed hearts, have been warned time and again from the earliest Teachings of Saint Germain not to gossip. If you do not believe that the Teaching is true, you may test the waters of your own life and experience firsthand the consequences of the lack of Abundance, the lack of Healing, the lack of Wholeness that will continue to permeate your life if you continue to engage in that negativity. That karmic reaction is not the Hand of God coming down as a hammer, as so many would like to think. It is the inescapable consequence of the misuse of the Light! And when you understand what is the misuse, what is the wise use, does it not merit your total attention to bring your consciousness into alignment with the Vibration of your Holy Christ Presence?

Do you suppose that any Ascended Master walking the Earth in their incarnations were not tested in this regard? Most assuredly they were. For it doesn't take long for the consequences of one's karma to teach a particular lesson.

Now you can say that you have the Decrees, the Violet Flame, the Emerald Ray, the Purity; you have the *Shekhinah Pillar*® to call upon. And indeed you do. But there does come the time when any misqualified activity is deliberately repeated, over and over again, that the Mighty I AM Presence desires and demands that you balance it by enduring the physical karmic recompense.

This is why there are some burdens that are no longer balanced by transmutation. For the opportunity has been given time and again, and yet, excuses were always made in the attitude "Thou shalt not surely die," as the serpent said in the Garden of Eden. You must realize, blessed ones, that the Truth of Cosmic Law is no respecter of persons.

We Hold Open Divine Opportunity

This coming Conclave[*] is an opportunity for you to recognize what is Holy, what is Divine, what is Perfect, what is the Vibration of Love, of caring, what allows for Wholeness to return not only to your life, but to the lives of the many that you serve with your Decrees, with your Service to God in life. It is an opportunity for you to move beyond the pettiness of your many incarnations and put on this Garment of the Christ.

But then, just as quickly as some have learned how the Light of God begins to flow through them, in a weakened state of consciousness, they fall back into the old patterns and habits. This is most unfortunate. For it takes an even greater impetus to overcome the next cycle, to rise beyond that vibration of negativity, and to recognize those patterns within one's world that require the Violet Flame, require the Light of God — but most importantly, the Christ Discernment not to enter into those patterns ever again! That is true Wisdom, beloved students of the Light. That is the wise initiate on the Path.

---

[*] *Harvest Conclave 2016: Royal Presence, Royal Mind II*

My counsel to you, as always, is to find your refuge, your safe haven within the Light of God. For your Mighty I AM Presence is always there, waiting for you to rise out of the murky waters of your human vibration and into the clarity of the Vision of your own Mighty I AM Presence.

This coming Conclave, as you heard from Beloved Virginia, is an opportunity for you to know more of the Emerald Ray. Perhaps you think you have already mastered it. Perhaps there is within your world the misconception that there is nothing more you can be taught, for surely your Presence has it all, and if you need to know it, your Presence will make it available to you. While that may be true, it is the wise Son or Daughter of God who hastens the day for the Wisdom to come forth and does not rely upon the possibility that at some point in the future you will stumble upon that Truth, that key to your own Divine Destiny!

We do not Come Merely for the Few, but for the Many

Why do you suppose the Ascended Masters have summoned you to gather together with these, our Anointed Representatives, as they lower not only the Teaching and Instruction from our Voice, but also our Momentum, and our very Presence into your midst? It is because, blessed ones, mankind, left to their own devices, was not accelerating on the Path. These, our Anointed Representatives, are a necessary requirement for our Light and Momentum to be lowered into each of the planes of consciousness, thereby radiating out so that the entire world may receive the Charge and Momentum of Truth and of Cosmic Law!

And while it does make a difference whether or not a handful of the students closest to this Fire are able to perceive and appropriate this Fire into their own lives, nonetheless, there are also those thousands of miles away who do not know that I, Mary, the Archeia of the Fifth Ray, am addressing the Earth this very hour! But they have received the Charge and a certain amount of the Instruction that has been lowered into the mental, emotional, and physical planes, that vibrates through Akasha. And they will register what they are capable of, according to their attainment.

This is how it works, blessed ones. We do not come merely for the few, but the many. And it is all-important for the Earth to have a firm foundation upon which the tide of the Golden River of the Helicon can continue to sweep the Earth with the very Living Presence of God so that the Golden Age will come, will manifest upon the Earth, and assist the Sons and Daughters of God to elevate into their Christhood.

Your Responsibility is to Put the Presence First

So you see, blessed ones, you do have a solemn Responsibility for what you say, what you do, the vibration of your countenance, and what you put first in your life. Is the Presence of God first? Is it the Light that is to go forth for the Earth? Is it the Teaching and Instruction that is to permeate the Earth? You will answer by your actions, by your vibration.

I, Mary, am constantly holding the Vision for you, each one, in the Immaculate Conception of your Christhood. I desire that you put away childish things. They are no longer cute. They no longer serve you well. And put on the Divinity of your Christhood! You are far and away mature enough to know who you are. Awaken to the Flame on the Altar of your Heart! Then you will know the Truth, know the Vibration of God that you desire to move within.

And if you do not desire to be in the Vibration of God, then, like it or not, you will gravitate to a level of association with the Ascended Masters in accordance with your vibration. If you desire to be a chela of one or more of the Ascended Masters, it takes great Fortitude, Courage, Strength! You must stand almost as though you are an Archeia or an Archangel in the countenance of your own Heart Flame so that you can move through the Initiations required. This Path is not for the weak! It is not for those who desire to hold on to their human creation.

Moving into the Realm of Christhood — as in the example of the many Ascended Masters who have gone before you — is a most challenging Initiation! But as you have come to know, it is worth every erg of energy that you must strive to bring to the fore. Master Morya is the greatest of Teachers when it comes to knowing how to strive for the Will of God. Saint Germain, one of the wisest Teachers, enables you to know the inner workings of the Divine Alchemy so that *you* can perform the Emerald Matrix in your life, you can satisfy Necessity's Ray!

So as you come to the Conclave, putting your attention upon your *Royal Presence, Royal Mind*, recognize that therein is the *key* to your Victory. You will want to be prepared so that the Strength, the Courage, and the Purity of your vibration is fully intact and ready for all the Ascended Masters have to share with you.

Come! Drink in the Emerald Ray! Let the Healing Current perform its Perfect Work in your life! At the close of the Conclave you will have accelerated your vehicles of consciousness into the Fullness that your Presence not only desires, but requires of you, so that you might fulfill the Fiery Destiny of this incarnation and not put off to another cycle what must be accomplished here and now.

Come, one and all, to put on the Garment of your Mighty I AM Presence as the Holy Christ Presence steps forth in the Emerald Ray!

I hold you in the Vision of Perfection so that you might attain to those vibrations required to fulfill your Fiery Destiny, here and now!

Mother Mary

Hail Mary

Healing

Hail Mary, Full of Grace,
The Lord is with thee.
O Sacred Heart of the Mother Flame,
Hold the Immaculate Vision
For us, the Sons and Daughters of God.

Holy Mary, Queen of Angels,
Hear our Call for Wholeness.
Pray for us now in our Victory,
Our Perfection and Ascension fulfilled.

Transmutation

Hail Mary, Full of Grace,
The Lord is with thee.
O Sacred Heart of the Mother Flame,
Hold the Immaculate Vision
For us, the Sons and Daughters of God.

Holy Mary, Queen of Angels,
Hear our Call for Violet Flame.
Pray for us now in our Victory,
Our Perfection and Ascension fulfilled.

We welcome you to become
a Torch Bearer of The Temple®
in a Sacred Covenant with
Beloved Saint Germain and
the Brotherhood's Mission through
The Temple of The Presence.®

If you would like more information on
becoming a Torch Bearer or on
The Temple of The Presence,
please call us at
520-751-2039
or visit our website at
www.templeofthepresence.org.

You are also invited to connect with us
on Facebook and Instagram.

We are so grateful you have heard
the Words of the Ascended Masters
and have recognized the Light of their
Consciousness going forth into the world.